NO YAMS YET!

Written by Dale Tenby

Illustrated by Gary Swift

Jim has a lot of yams.

3

The yams go in the van.
But the van can not go.

No yams yet!

Viv tuts.
Viv is fed up.

Wez jogs up.
He can get the van to go.

Wez revs the van.

The van zig zags up.
Viv gets the yams!